Live for the Soul

Vanessa Stone

in remembrance of the One.

Vanessa Stone is a teacher and humanitarian.

Her teachings inspire the realization that there is no true
separation. She shares that life is the spiritual path
and all beings have direct contact with what is
real and alive at the heart of creation.

Within immersion retreat settings, Vanessa often writes
personalized entries in participant journals. These writings
serve to stoke the fire of self-inquiry and bring deeper
awareness to each individual's intimate spiritual journey.
The following writings are excerpts from these entries.

This book speaks authentically to the human condition:
it is a tool of remembrance, offered
in the spirit of contemplation.

This book is not intended to be read cover to cover:
it is arranged as a series of individual inquiries,
and can be opened at random, as inspired.

You can use the facing page of each inquiry to journal
your own reflections as you move through the book.

We offer you this small book of inspiration and guidance
with great love, and a true wish for you to thrive.

May you live for the soul.

Your Life, exactly as it is, is the perfect prescription for the evolution of your soul.

It contains all that is essential in realizing God - in making God real - within every speck and expression of creation, throughout the human condition and woven into everyday life.

This is an invitation to deepen into the heart of Living, to return to what is essential: to redefine the purpose of this Life and realize the Gift within this human experience.

Life is the spiritual path.

Receive this life anew...
the way it was intended to be...
free from your imaginary limitations...
an open sea of possibilities...

The Beloved's dream for you.

Welcome home.

There is an open window... a vantage
point into a chamber of your heart that
exists without expectation or conditions...

it is open for all being,
known and unknown...

but first...
you have to see *your Self*
through this window.

Move with the grace of The Way.

Offer your tender heart as a temple for The One.

There is no other.

You are The One...
one with The Way.

Listen to the bird song... become the fragrance... polish the mirror of your Heart to reflect the light of Truth within creation.

This has been the sacred gift of your innocent mother... your medicine.

For if in this lifetime the yearning to be loved was not so strong, you may never have realized the Infinite Love...
free from obligation...
free from human conditions.

Your mother has become a servant for your return.

She led you... innocently.

Unshroud your essence...
Mother to the world.

Your light is not delicate...
it does not need to be veiled.

Beyond unmet expectations,
judgment and the fears
of being weak,
of being nothing...

there is Life...

free from these conditions.

See through the eye of your heart...

Allow outcomes to be revealed...

Walk with open hands, empty cup...

Read the Living Map.

All life is pointing you home.

Bow to the moment...
become the movement...
malleable again... as before you were
born.

You were born from higher vision...
infused with the sight of the One that
dreamed Creation.

In the illusion of separation, this was
forgotten.

In the willingness to return to Truth,
remembrance is restored... restoration from
fragmentation.

You have passed the point of no return.

Surrender the struggle... collapse if you have to... be carried by the wisdom of experience and allow it to teach you.

Walk into the dwelling place... allow God to caress your beautiful face.

Stop looking for right and wrong... free yourself from the burden of keeping justice.

Trust Nature's Way... the alchemy of experience and its intelligent design.

Grace is present.

There comes a time when the
relationship with God transforms
from that of parent and child
into the partnership of Lovers.

Where prayers are no longer from the
eyes of a child looking up... but from the
impassioned lover looking into the eyes
of the Beloved, with an invitation to
make love... to create and be united in
creation.

The hand is extended...

Be the Bride of the Beloved,
and fall naked and drunk...

It is already written...
you need "know" nothing more.

You are The Beloved's sweetheart...

You initiated the quest to discover what is true, essential, and untouched by time...

Appreciate impermanence and rest in what does not waver...

Pure, present, alive...

Truth.

Look towards the temple within.

Tend to the temple... devote your
attention again and again to its sacred
space... invoke the light of your
awareness to inhabit this space once
again.

Turn in toward the temple of the soul
and drink from the cup of sweet mercy
for your wandering... simply to return...
again and again.

The door is wide open...

Come, as you are.

How does the heart know to beat?
How does the moon know when to
wane? How does a flower turn to fruit?
How will you know when to let go?

Trust what is most naturally occurring...
unified with The Force.

Commune. Attune to the subtle.

The variety of fruit in our garden is
infinite... every moment offers a different
taste... make no separation between bitter
and sweet.

This is a garden of experience...
ever deepening experience of
The Beloved...

bitter, sweet and beyond...
study what offers plenty...
nourish self, nourish others.

This love...
intelligent, infinite supply.

Worshiping thoughts and beliefs
is the root of human suffering.

Mind fixates on the preservation
of its own images...

especially the often complicated image
of "me" and what "I" need.

What we think of
is removed
from what is occurring now:

Reality.

Unite with Reality,
and reclaim the mind as an instrument...
release it from being a God.

Cultivate a devotional mind...
study Nature and its ways.

Awaken to what is being offered in its simplicity... give up on trying to exchange the offering for something more familiar to you... for that which satisfies your senses or supports your images of how you wish to be perceived.

The power is in your willingness...

In that which causes you to take deep breaths... signs from the letting go.

Deep Breath.

Recognize the place beyond
"right and wrong," "good and bad,"
"powerful and not powerful,"
"important and unimportant."

Freedom is here.
Pure movement is here.

You are *here*.

Live with no clothes on.

Be.

There is a revolution of the Soul...
a returning to a more tender time...
where vulnerability, receptivity,
and a willingness to explore
the intricacies of your heart
is paramount.

Let your Heart breathe...
give voice to the whispering within...
declare your longing.

Erase the images and clear your eyes to
see the Beloved standing before you...
begging for your naked awareness.

Respond.

Every moment is a meeting with
God...with Self, the Beloved disguised in
infinite forms... be it a child, a fleet of
soldiers, a suffering animal or a tree
bearing fruit and flowers.

There is no separation... only a world
seen through the many filters of the
human story, be it through the veiled
heart or the eyes of an awakened master.

At the root of this apparent world there
is only Love, Pure God, waiting to be
met in a moment when the seduction of
this apparition is transcended by the
longing for conscious communion.

Receptive mind...
naked Heart.

Consciousness moves through you...
and through all being...
Awake.

Open the door... let the world in.

What is being offered cannot be taken.

Rest...
settle in...
grow roots.

There is a place inside of you
that remains undiscovered.

There is Sanctuary at your core...
the place where there is only God...
without form, without limitation.

Live to be fully awake in each and every moment.

The presence that you are becomes an invitation for all of humanity to come into deep conscious communion with the living essence of God.

Actualize communion.

The work is over...
your soul can breathe.

This is no longer an arduous path of
opening. You must stop all trying...
there is nothing left undone.

Open your eyes and notice the Heart of
the One is the foundation of your living.

Cease the effort to be any *more*
devoted... you have already been
devoured.

Wake up to this Truth and swim in the
Ocean of The Way.

Witness Grace... notice the workings...
and simply pray to rest into this life...
to be as you are... within *This*.

Now is the time to spiritually engage
with Life... to have the courage to
commit to bringing conscious
recognition of the Unity to daily
living... to have the courage to allow
all structures that are unsustainable -
rooted in fear and separation - to fall
away.

Allow...
a pause between promises...
a space to explore the momentum of
creative inspiration...
allow all ideas to enter into "the
pause," so they can be washed in the
highest intelligence...
clarified with the gaze of God...

so that you can respond in full
recognition of what truly serves
The Whole.

You are no longer a seeker.

From here on...
there is no more looking.

It is here.

What is being offered?

Listen, feel...
use all your senses.

The beginning ends here.

So the stream of a million doors is open...
each one a deeper glimpse into what has
been offered again and again...
form after form, teacher after teacher,
illness after illness, child after child.

And now, the final door, the door in
the secret heart, illuminated...
radiant invitation.

This door before you now, the one you
prayed for: the one that can only be
opened with your own willingness.

Now is the time to pour all grievances
at the feet of God... to crawl like a
hungry beggar if you must... no wound is
too deep... all is welcomed here.

This time your prayers are being carried by your own heart... your heart is the vehicle for this return.

This heart, alive in you... unveiled... discovered... is carrying the medicine for your humanity. Your body contains your heart... your heart contains the soul... the soul contains the medicine... the elixir for liberated loving... freedom beyond measure.

You hear the call... you cannot resist... give it all... this whisper is actualized as the most glorious *yes*.

Welcome home Beloved one...
welcome to the place where all paths end.

This is only about the posture in which you arrive to this moment.

There is never an absence of God, of Grace...

the only thing that wanders is your attention.

Be aware of silence.
Commune with stillness.

Experience the most subtle...
the most potent medicine.

God is a living essence within you, a heart within a heart, longing to be realized.

Trust in the intelligent design of nature... as it moves through each one of us, revealing itself, shaping us, driving us into being... beyond our highest expectations...

Hand over the outcomes and become deeply immersed in this offering.

Allow Grace.

There is a place within you that is fully awake, authentically at peace, liberated and fully aware of this creation called "your life" and the immense opportunity it offers the Soul.

Live for the Soul.

Vanessa Stone is a teacher, humanitarian, alchemist, artist, leader for peace and Founder of the Amala Foundation, a non-profit organization working to create sustainable peace within and without.

Vanessa has devoted her life to humanitarian service and sharing her message of realizing God through the study of Nature. She teaches that "your Life is the spiritual path," and inspires individuals and communities to unite in peace and loving service. Vanessa has deeply touched the lives of many through her direct guidance, compassionate listening and unwavering devotion. She shares her message through private sessions, public sittings, silent retreats, residential immersions, and international service missions.

In 2002 Vanessa founded the Amala Foundation, which works to create a peaceful, equitable and compassionate world by unifying communities in service, inspiring youth to lead with a heart-centered global perspective, and living in recognition that sustainable peace begins within.

The Amala Foundation has successfully initiated a wide range of humanitarian projects, including the Global Youth Peace Summit, Bhatti Mines School Project in India, Sustainable Village Water Project in Africa, the International Children's Peace Exchange, Camp Indigo, Camp Mana, Prison Peace Project, and the One Village Project.

Vanessa travels around the world sharing her message of sustainable peace and serving a global community through the many projects of the Amala Foundation. Contact us to find out more about Vanessa's work:

Offerings@VanessaStone.org
www.AmalaFoundation.org
www.VanessaStone.org
800-476-1148

Made in the USA
Charleston, SC
17 March 2012